TURNING POINTS

THE RISE OF SOCIAL MEDIA

BY JIM WHITING

CREATIVE EDUCATION • CREATIVE PAPERBACKS

Published by Creative Education and Creative Paperbacks
P.O. Box 227, Mankato, Minnesota 56002
Creative Education and Creative Paperbacks are imprints of
The Creative Company
www.thecreativecompany.us

Design by The Design Lab
Production by Colin O'Dea
Art direction by Rita Marshall
Printed in China

Photographs by Alamy (AKP Photos, Richard Levine), Creative Commons
Wikimedia (G. F. and E. B. Bensell, Magnus Manske/Tekniska museet,
Ferdinand Pauwels, Anthony Quintano, Rama & Musée Bolo, Evan Williams),
Getty Images (Daniel Berehulak/Getty Images Sport, Owen Franken/
Corbis Documentary, Dimitri Otis/Photographer's Choice , Steve Proehl/
Corbis Documentary), iStockphoto (amesy, Aunt_Spray, DGLimages, ipopba,
jacoblund, JRLPhotographer, lenalir, mediaphotos, Milan_Jovic, Montes-Bradley,
Pgiam, santypan, scisettialfio)

Library of Congress Cataloging-in-Publication Data
Names: Whiting, Jim, author.
Title: The rise of social media / Jim Whiting.
Series: Turning points.
Includes bibliographical references and index.
Summary: A historical account of the social media boom, including the
technological advancements that enabled widespread Internet use, the people
involved, how companies such as Facebook and Twitter capitalized on it, and
the lingering aftermath.
Identifiers: ISBN 978-1-64026-176-1 (hardcover) / ISBN 978-1-62832-739-7
(pbk) / ISBN 978-1-64000-294-4 (eBook)
This title has been submitted for CIP processing under LCCN 2019935431.

CCSS: RI.5.1, 2, 3, 8; RI. 6.1, 2, 4, 7; RH.6–8.3, 4, 5, 6, 7, 8

First Edition HC 9 8 7 6 5 4 3 2 1
First Edition PBK 9 8 7 6 5 4 3 2 1

TABLE *of* CONTENTS

Social media surrounds us. People in virtually every corner of the globe have their own Facebook page. Twitter allows us to let friends know what we are doing in real time or to follow interesting people. YouTube videos draw us into watching the antics of almost every kind of animal for hours. We regularly check our e-mail, too. Many of us wouldn't dream of leaving home without a smartphone to stay connected.

Starting in the mid-1990s, Internet-based social media began to form an important part of people's lives. Now, more than 20 years later, social media in all its many manifestations has profoundly changed the ways in which people all over the world interact. This transformation over such a short period of time has come with both benefits and drawbacks. The rise of social media has truly become a turning point in world history.

Posting selfies to social media has become commonplace, but the motivations behind selfie-taking is an area of interest to psychologists today.

Before fountain pens with nibs were mass-produced in the 1820s, people who used dip pens for personal correspondence had to be able to afford the necessary ink and quills.

CHAPTER ONE

GETTING SOCIAL

People have always been social creatures. We want to communicate with each other and stay in touch. Many people think that social media began in the latter part of the 20th century. But its roots go back thousands of years. One of the original forms of written communication was the letter. People not only wrote to each other, but they also marked their letters and shared them with others. For short distances, letters could be exchanged by people who were on foot. If they had to travel longer distances, letters could be carried by horses or ships. Either way, it was a relatively cumbersome process of communication.

Social media users today post messages on a digital "wall." That concept is based on real walls. In Roman times, people wrote notes to each other and posted them on the walls and doors of their homes as well as the homes of others. A church door played a key role in social networking in 1517. German priest Martin Luther was upset with many of the practices of the Roman Catholic Church. He made a list of those practices he disagreed with in what became known as the 95 Theses. Then he posted them on a

Fountain pen nib

Legends about Luther's posting of his questions and topics for debate are more dramatic than the likely reality of his hanging a notice of scholarly discussion in a public place.

OFF WITH HIS HAND!

An early form of government regulation of social media occurred in 1579. English Queen Elizabeth was considering a marriage with the brother of the King of France. The primary reason was political. The marriage would unite the two countries against Spain. An English lawyer named John Stubbs wrote a political pamphlet that opposed the marriage. After it was published, many people throughout England read the pamphlet and commented on it. Elizabeth was outraged. She ordered Stubbs to be arrested. After a quick trial, he was found guilty. His punishment was having his right hand amputated. It was the one he had used to write the critique.

church door. They were quickly printed and, as we might say today, "went viral." A friend of Luther's wrote that "hardly fourteen days had passed when these propositions were known throughout Germany and within four weeks almost all of Christendom was familiar with them." Posting and publishing the 95 Theses led to the Protestant Reformation—a landmark event in world history that marked the division of Christianity into Catholics and Protestants.

In the 17th century, another early form of social media emerged with the rise of European coffeehouses. Today's coffee shops attract customers who spend their time hunched over laptops or phones. But early coffeehouses were lively assemblages of people discussing the issues of the day. Many of these discussions centered on politics. In that era, political pamphlets and newspapers enjoyed wide circulation and provided plenty to talk about. The coffeehouses also served as a kind of post office, where people could mail letters or pick them up. In some cases, they even served as commercial centers. The famous insurance company Lloyd's of London got its start in a coffeehouse owned by Edward Lloyd, with a concentration on **maritime** matters.

Not everyone approved of the coffeehouse culture. In 1673, an anonymous author wrote one of the first criticisms of social media. He called coffeehouses "an exchange, where **haberdashers** of political small-wares meet, and mutually abuse each other, and the publick, with bottomless stories, and headless notions; the rendezvous of idle pamphlets, and persons more idly employed to read them." Still, people continued to gather in coffeehouses and cafes, sharing ideas and building new ones on top of them.

This was the situation well into the 19th century. Whether in coffeehouses or through written correspondence, many social interactions were conducted face-to-face or via personal letters.

The Morse Code

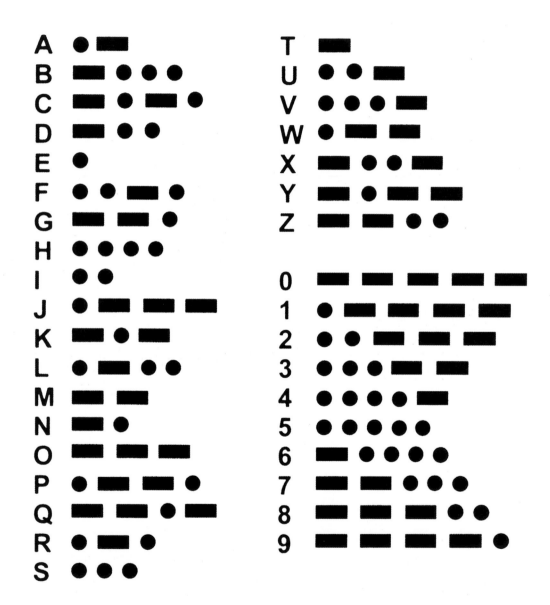

As is the case today with online communications, parents often tried to exert control over the letters their children sent and received. In one notable case, the future horror writer Edgar Allan Poe had secretly become engaged to a young woman. Her father disapproved of the engagement. So he intercepted Poe's letters and burned them. Because she never received the letters, she felt that Poe no longer cared for her. She soon married another young man.

The invention of a simplified version of the **telegraph** by Samuel F. B. Morse in the 1840s marked a major change in communication methods. Messages were no longer limited to the speed of a ship on the open seas or a person walking or riding a horse. Now they zipped back and forth along telegraph lines. In ideal conditions, they could be delivered to the recipient within a few minutes of being sent. In a short time, much of the United States was linked by telegraph wires. "It is anticipated that the whole of the populous parts of the United States

Samuel F. B. Morse

will, within two or three years, be covered with a net-work like a spider's web," wrote one observer in 1848. Messages were transmitted via Morse code, in which letters are represented by combinations of short and long signals (and written as dots and dashes). In an early version of present-day texting, telegraph operators adopted abbreviations to simplify things and speed up transmissions. Thus, "gm" stood for "good morning" and "sfd" was short for "stop for dinner."

A short time after Morse patented the electric telegraph, more than 50 companies were supplying telegraph keys and other equipment around the U.S.

In 1858, the first **transatlantic** cable was laid. The world was becoming fully wired. Five years later, noted science fiction author Jules Verne—whose subjects included globe-circling submarines and humans landing on the moon long before either of these achievements was a reality—predicted a future in which "photo-telegraphy allowed any writing, signature, or illustration to be sent faraway—every house was wired."

Telegraph operators formed their own social networks. During times when they had no messages to send, they chatted amongst themselves, told jokes, and even played games like checkers and chess using the telegraph lines. And sometimes they even fell in love, thanks to 19th-century instant messaging.

The rise of mass communication in the late 1800s and early 1900s changed the social media landscape even further. It began with mass-circulation newspapers, then telephone, radio, and finally television. These new media provided instant communication over long distances. However, only a few people could afford to own them. And most of the communication was one-way. There was little interaction between media distributors and recipients.

Yet another technological form arose in the 1930s. Large computing machines sometimes filled entire rooms. World War II accelerated the development of these machines as warring nations sought technological advantages over their enemies. Computer research continued after the end of the war with the onset of the Cold War, when the U.S. and its allies experienced tense relations with the Soviet Union and its allies. This research took on a special urgency for the U.S. in 1957.

POINTING OUT

I TAKE THEE …

*In the mid-1840s, a woman fell in love with Mr. B., a man who worked in her father's business in Boston. Her father disapproved. He sent the man on a voyage to England. Mr. B.'s ship stopped in New York before crossing the Atlantic. The young woman sent him a message: Be at the telegraph office in New York with a **magistrate** at a certain time. He did as the woman directed. She was in the Boston telegraph office. The magistrate performed the wedding vows, which hummed over the telegraph lines. Her father was upset. But the marriage was legally binding. It is perhaps the first example of an "online" marriage.*

Early computational machines, primarily meant for performing calculations and decoding communications, gave rise to the term "computer."

CHAPTER TWO

NETWORKING MEDIA

O n October 4, 1957, the Soviet Union launched *Sputnik 1*. The size of a basketball, it was the first artificial satellite placed into Earth's orbit. Although its scientific value was minimal, it prompted a national outcry in America. The U.S. was lagging behind its adversary in the Cold War.

One early response was the formation of the Defense Advanced Research Projects Agency (DARPA). It used several massive computers. During the 1960s, the agency's scientists searched for a way to allow those computers to "speak" to one another. The result was the first computer network, ARPANET, established in 1969 to connect four computers. Many more computers were added to ARPANET during the 1970s.

But as the network grew, it became increasingly difficult for the machines to communicate. Computer scientist Vinton Cerf solved the problem about a decade later. He established the Transmission Control Protocol (TCP), and then added the Internet Protocol (IP). Together, these protocols have been described as "the 'handshake' that introduces distant and different computers to each other in a virtual space." As a result, Cerf is often called the "father of the Internet."

By then, one of the most important developments in computer history

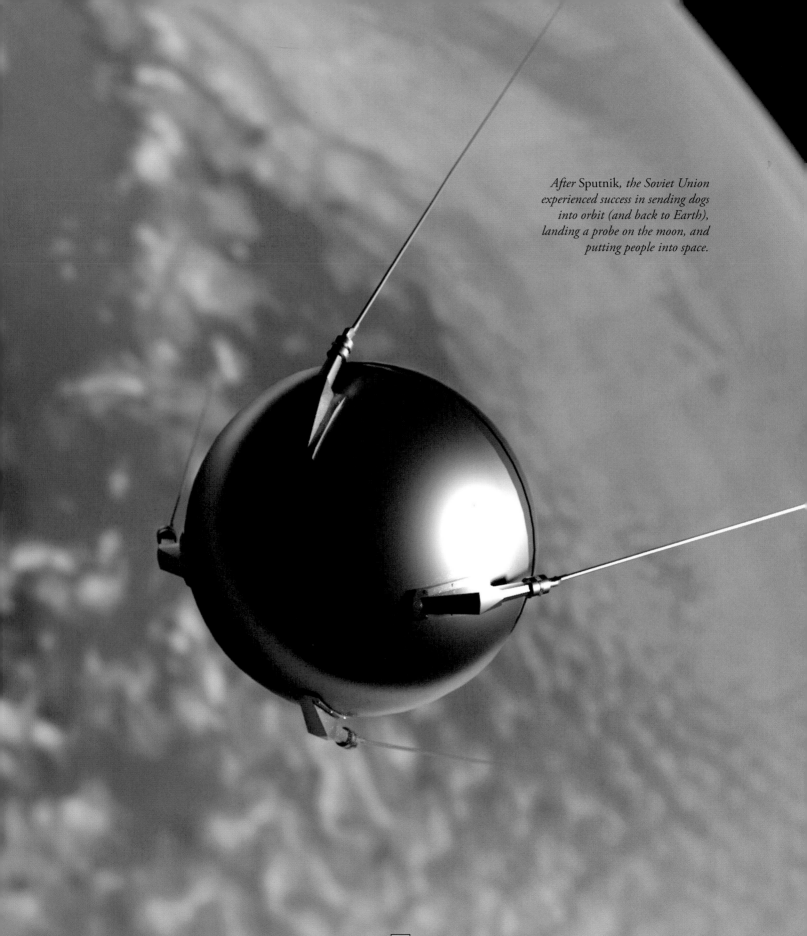

After Sputnik, *the Soviet Union experienced success in sending dogs into orbit (and back to Earth), landing a probe on the moon, and putting people into space.*

was underway: the production of lighter-weight and less expensive personal computers. Scaling down the machines made it possible for more people to own them. The three main components—the monitor, the central processing unit, and the keyboard—usually fit easily on a table or desktop.

Personal computers were designed to be easy to operate. That allowed millions of people without a technical background to use them. At first, personal computers were used primarily to play games and complete word-processing tasks. Many new computer owners also dialed into bulletin board systems that allowed them to exchange messages with one another. Companies such as CompuServe and America Online (AOL) offered **dial-up** services such as e-mail. For many people, e-mail was a huge step forward. It was instantaneous. It allowed people to bypass the long process of writing letters, putting them into envelopes, mailing them, and waiting days or even longer for a response.

Eventually, it became possible to access the Internet with personal computers. But it was usually a slow process, well beyond the reach of people without specialized computer skills. That was about to change. In 1990, Tim Berners-Lee, a physicist with the European Organization for Nuclear Research (CERN), wrote a program called the World Wide Web. The Web, as it is often called, is not the same thing as the Internet. The Internet is a global network of computers. The Web is a collection of an estimated 15 to 30 billion pages, all of which begin with the familiar http protocol: http:// www.

Berners-Lee's original intention was simply to allow his fellow scientists to communicate more easily with each other. Aided by Mosaic—the first

browser to simplify Internet searches—the Web came into widespread, free use in 1993. As Berners-Lee explained, "Originally I wanted it to be the medium by which I could share ideas with people, so it was very much supposed to be a collaborative medium."

The online population exploded. Millions of people created personal web pages that were accessible to anyone. The next step was combining these pages into a network. SixDegrees.com is widely regarded as the first social networking site. The name comes from the phrase "six degrees of separation," a theory that every person on Earth can be linked to anyone else through a chain of six acquaintances between them. The theory was first proposed in the 1920s. It became popular in 1990 with playwright John Guare's play *Six Degrees of Separation* and a film of the same name three years later. A character says, "I find it extremely comforting that we're so close. I also find it like Chinese water torture, that we're so close because you have to find the right six people to make the right connection … I am bound, you are bound, to everyone on this planet by a trail of six people."

That seemed like a good omen for a site that was trying to bring people together, regardless of where they lived. When it was launched in 1997, the site included profiles and lists of

Children of the 1990s who had access to school computer labs learned how to type and played educational games to supplement their studies.

friends. Visitors to someone's site could click on any of that person's friends. However, it lacked the capability to post pictures. Even though it had more than a million members by 2000, it wasn't commercially successful. It soon shut down.

The next social network was Friendster, founded in 2002 as a social networking and gaming site. It quickly caught on. Media publicity generated millions of new users. But the system couldn't handle the influx. Pages sometimes took nearly a minute to download. Rather than deal with service issues, its founders devoted their

POINTING OUT

SIX DEGREES OF KEVIN BACON

In a 1994 magazine interview, noted film actor Kevin Bacon discussed the vast number of people with whom he had worked in Hollywood. Influenced by the theory of six degrees of separation, which had recently become popular, four college students created a game they called Six Degrees of Kevin Bacon. A book and websites soon followed. All showed the connections between Bacon and people in the film industry. At first Bacon disliked the idea. He thought it was ridiculing him. He eventually changed his mind. In 2007, Bacon founded the charity SixDegrees.org. It links celebrities with charities.

Chris DeWolfe, Tom Anderson, and other colleagues from the Internet marketing company eUniverse cofounded MySpace and sold it for $580 million.

attention to installing new features—which slowed the website even more.

A different approach to social networking came with the launch of LinkedIn in 2003. It was originally intended as a method for jobseekers to post resumes. It soon became a way for professionals to interact with others in their respective fields. It also became useful for recruiters, who could list job openings. It continues to thrive and grow by adding new features. For example, high school students can create LinkedIn profiles to include with their college applications. For security, LinkedIn has adopted the "gated-access approach." Access to someone on the site requires an existing relationship or an "introduction" through one of that person's contacts.

The first big social network, MySpace, was also founded in 2003. MySpace attracted Friendster users who were growing frustrated with its problems. "Users at Friendster could view only the profiles of those on a relatively short chain of acquaintances," according to the *New York Times*. "By contrast, MySpace was open, and therefore much simpler from a technological standpoint; anybody could look at anyone else's profile." Within three years, it had become the top-rated social network. As its peak, according to *Vanity Fair*, "Each day, 170,000 new members sign up, creating their own pages, filling out profiles, uploading photos, and linking to an extended network of like-minded others. The average MySpace user spends over two hours a month on the site." But MySpace's reign was brief. A social network destined to become far larger and more pervasive was on the horizon.

POINTING OUT

FACT—OR FICTION?

*Is something on social media a fact or a hoax? Snopes.com can be helpful in deciding. Based in Tacoma, Washington, Snopes is the best-known fact-checking site in the U.S. Its CEO, David Mikkelson, employs more than a dozen people to determine what is real and what isn't. Snopes leaped into prominence after the 9/11 attacks. "Conspiracy theories were running rampant," says Mikkelson. "We were the only ones cataloging what was true or not." Another spike came when Barack Obama ran for president in 2008. "Everything went crazy," he said, as Snopes **debunked** claims such as "Obama is a Muslim."*

CHAPTER THREE

BIRTH OF THE GIANTS

The story of Facebook began early in 2004 in a **dormitory** room at Harvard University, in Cambridge, Massachusetts. At that time, many colleges had picture directories of students, which included basic information, such as phone numbers. Some referred to them as "face books." Harvard didn't have a face book. Sophomore Mark Zuckerberg was quoted in the school's newspaper as saying, "Everyone's been talking a lot about a universal face book within Harvard.... I think it's kind of silly that it would take the University a couple of years to get around to it. I can do it better than they can, and I can do it in a week."

Zuckerberg hacked into the school's student records. His first creation was Facemash. It showed a series of pages of two students side by side. Viewers judged the attractiveness of the people in the photos. Nearly 500 people logged on to Facemash in the next few hours. The school shut it down after two days.

Harvard University

That didn't stop Zuckerberg. He set up what he called thefacebook.com. It included a **template** that allowed students

Even though Mark Zuckerberg dropped out of Harvard to launch Facebook, the university granted him an honorary degree in 2017.

In 2018, Facebook added a 525,000-square-foot building to its already expansive campus to house approximately 3,000 employees.

to fill in their own information. The site went live on February 4. Within a month, much of Harvard's student population had joined. Other schools quickly showed interest. By May, the site included at least 30 more schools.

Then Zuckerberg traveled to Palo Alto, California. He originally intended to stay for the summer and return to Harvard in the fall. But while in California, he met some venture capitalists. These are people with substantial amounts of money who want to fund **entrepreneurs** with promising ideas.

Zuckerberg attracted a backer. He decided not to go back to Harvard. He was taking the advice of another noted Harvard dropout: Microsoft cofounder Bill Gates. Zuckerberg once attended a presentation by Gates at Harvard. Gates told his audience to take as much time off from school as they needed to pursue interests that might amount to something.

Armed with his newfound cash, Zuckerberg devoted his time to his **fledgling** project. He went into high gear. He hired engineers and programmers. Early in 2005, Zuckerberg dropped "The" from the company name. Now it was just Facebook. That fall, he opened the site to high school students. The following year, anyone age 13 or older with a valid e-mail address could join. Membership mushroomed. In 2008, Facebook overtook MySpace as the top-rated social media site, with an estimated 100 million users. Today, estimates range as high as 2 billion.

Twitter, another giant Internet site, was launched in 2006. Its cofounders, Jack Dorsey and Evan Williams, realized that status updates would be much more practical if they could be refreshed while members were away from their computers. So Twitter began operations with mobile phone applications. It benefited from the introduction of the iPhone in

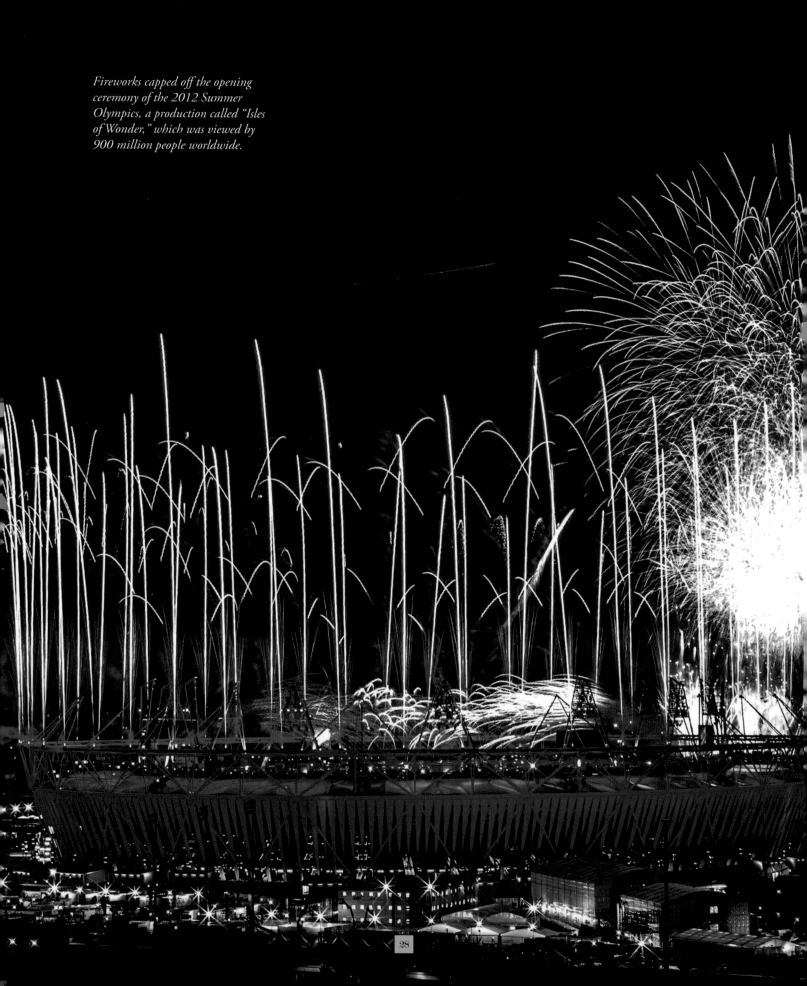

Fireworks capped off the opening ceremony of the 2012 Summer Olympics, a production called "Isles of Wonder," which was viewed by 900 million people worldwide.

POINTING OUT

LIGHTING THE OLYMPIC TWEET

Organizers of the Opening Ceremonies of the 2012 London Olympics wanted to emphasize that the digital revolution was as important historically as the 18th-century Industrial Revolution. They gave World Wide Web founder Tim Berners-Lee an important role. The audience saw Berners-Lee live-tweet "This is for everyone." His message zipped around the stadium. "The values and achievements of the Olympics will be amplified by the World Wide Web," he said. "It will be like millions of digital torches carrying the spirit of the Games to every corner of the world. It is an honour to have played a part for such an inspiring and truly international event."

2007 and the Android operating system soon afterward. Those smartphones led to an explosive growth for mobile phones using both platforms. Now users could stay in touch as long as they had cell phone reception.

Dorsey explained the origin of the site's name. "We wanted to capture that feeling: the physical sensation that you're buzzing your friend's pocket.... We came across the word 'twitter,' and it was just perfect. The definition was 'a short burst of inconsequential information,' and 'chirps from

Twitter cofounders Jack Dorsey and Evan Williams remained actively involved with the company—until Williams left the board of directors in February 2019.

birds.' And that's exactly what the product was." He added, "On Twitter, you're not watching the person, you're watching what they produce. There's no real social pressure inherent in having to call them a 'friend' ... because you're not dealing with them personally, you're dealing with what they've put out there."

For technical reasons, the total length of each tweet could not exceed 160 characters. Of those, 20 were reserved for the user name and routing information. That left 140 characters for the

POINTING OUT

THE ARAB SPRING

The Arab Spring began in Tunisia late in 2010 and quickly spread to other Arab countries. It was a revolt against oppressive **regimes**. *Social media played a key role in its growth. Protesters created new Facebook pages and used them to coordinate demonstrations. Tweets flooded Twitter and helped demonstrators stay in touch with one another. Unfortunately, the Arab Spring didn't result in an increase in democracy. But it did show the power of social media. According to a University of Washington study, "Our evidence suggests that social media carried a cascade of messages about freedom and democracy across North Africa and the Middle East, and helped raise expectations for the success of political uprising."*

message itself. Users began retweeting and using hashtags. Within six years, Twitter had generated more than 200 million users. In November 2017, Twitter doubled the number of allowable characters, to 280.

Commentators have compared Twitter with the **Roman Forum** or the *agora*—the central marketplace—of Greek city-states. Twitter allows users to exchange news and opinions directly with each other rather than relying on outside sources. Author Tom Standage observes that Twitter is more immediate and conversational than other social media outlets. Users can engage in a running commentary on everything from entertainment to world politics. In addition, "Twitter users can assemble their own personal feeds of information from friends, celebrities, and institutions such as government agencies, companies, and newspapers."

In 2005, Jawed Karim, Chad Hurley, and Steve Chen created a video-sharing site to make it easier to obtain and share videos. The site became known as YouTube. Their first video was called, "Me at the Zoo." It showed Karim in front of the elephant enclosure at the San Diego Zoo. Karim spent 19 seconds talking about the animals' trunks. Five months later, YouTube had its first one-million-views video. In it, Brazilian soccer star Ronaldinho puts on a pair of Nike Air Tiempo soccer shoes and (perhaps with the aid of some camera trickery) manages to keep the ball off the ground for more than a minute—including four consecutive **caroms** off the goal crossbar that bounce right back to him. Recognizing its growth and potential, Google purchased YouTube for $1.65 billion in 2006. Today it is has more than a billion users, who watch millions of hours' worth of videos about cats, home improvement, sports highlights, and more.

Instagram was founded in 2010. Its name is a combination of instant camera and telegram—a nod to the first electronic medium. Facebook purchased the social service in 2012. Other popular social media sites include Snapchat, Reddit, Tumblr, Flickr, and Pinterest. More pop up all the time. Many people belong to multiple sites as the influence of social media becomes increasingly important in everyday life.

Social media users upload 300 hours' worth of videos to YouTube every minute, hoping to be the next "stars" to earn a living hosting videos.

CHAPTER FOUR

PLEASURES AND PERILS

In just a short period of time—about 20 years—social media companies have expanded their reach and influence to every corner of the globe. There are many benefits of this expansion. It's easy to reach out to someone almost anywhere in the world. You can stay in touch with your friends, no matter where they are. You can comment on what they post, and you can read their comments on yours. It may be exciting to post something and see how many people "Like" it.

Whether you are in front of your computer or away from home, you and your friends can connect via Twitter or social messaging apps such as Facebook Messenger or Google Hangouts. Many people have had the pleasant experience of unexpectedly hearing from someone with whom they had lost touch years or even decades earlier.

It's also easier to stay in touch with the wider world. You don't need to wait for formal newscasts or newspaper delivery. Social media has instant information on what's happening, and your friends will provide commentary and links to sites you may not be familiar with.

Businesses love social media. It provides an easy and relatively low-cost way of reaching out to new and existing customers. Many business sites are entirely online and have the capability of precisely targeting their ads to

Remote-communication applications enable military personnel to stay in touch with their families back home when they are stationed elsewhere.

maximize the potential return.

But the rise of social media has had a number of negative effects. The horrific shooting at a Jewish synagogue in Pittsburgh just before the 2018 midterm elections showed one of the dark sides. It released a flood of **anti-Semitism**. Within a few days, more than 11,000 posts had the hashtag #jewsdid911, in a totally unfounded claim that Jews were responsible for the terrorist attacks of September 11, 2001. "Social media companies have created, allowed, and enabled **extremists** to move their message from the margins to the mainstream," said Jonathan Greenblatt of the Anti-Defamation League, a

POINTING OUT

RAPPING FOR RECRUITS

*An unusual use of social media is jihadi rap. Videos with extremist Islamic ideals expressed through rap have popped up on the Internet. "This is an effort ... to make these groups more approachable to potential recruits in places like Britain or France or America who are **susceptible** to rap videos but who might feel that the beheading videos we've seen in the past are too extreme," said CNN counterterrorism expert Philip Mudd. American-born Omar Hammami made the **genre** more popular with his video, "Blow by Blow." The music appeals to listeners who might feel oppressed or wronged by society.*

One of the dangers of instantaneous posting to social media is the difficulty in vetting claims rapidly enough to prevent the spread of misinformation.

DAILY NEWS

Anguish is etched on face of woman outside Pittsburgh temple where Robert Bowers (below) killed 11 people Saturday during Sabbath prayers.

PAGES 4-6

TEMPLE MASSACRE

Anti-Semitic

group that combats hate speech. "In the past, they couldn't find audiences for their poison. Now, with a click or a post or a tweet, they can spread their ideas with a velocity we've never seen before."

The sheer volume of daily postings complicates efforts to identify and remove hate speech and deliberate lies. According to Facebook, its internal systems flagged less than 40 percent of hate speech on the site in 2018. In comparison, those systems identified more than 99 percent of terrorist content. At the same time, YouTube users flagged millions of videos that they felt violated community guidelines. The site's automated tools took down 6.8 million more. But no one believes that these methods achieved anywhere near 100 percent success. A 2018 study by researchers at the Massachusetts Institute of Technology showed that Twitter users were 70 percent more likely to retweet untruths than accurate information.

Cyberbullying is one of the most negative aspects of social media. In one survey, more than one-third of middle school students reported that they had been the victims of cyberbullying. Girls are more likely to encounter it. Cyberbullying takes numerous forms. Some of the most common include attacking people online because of their looks, spreading false and malicious rumors, and posting mean-spirited comments intended to be damaging. Others are threats of actual physical violence, hurtful pictures, and pretending to be someone else online. Attacks because of race, religion or sexual orientation are especially common. The results of cyberbullying can be severe. Many victims feel a loss of self-esteem, while some turn to self-harming behavior. Even more frightening, a significant number succumb to suicidal thoughts. Some try to carry out those thoughts. In a few cases, they are successful.

Another negative effect prevalent among teens is a link between social media participation—especially on smartphones—and depression. According to a 2018 study, this link coincides with increased use of smartphones among teens during the second decade of the 21st century and helps explain a 50 percent increase in depressive episodes during that time. "The largest change and most pervasive change in teens' lives was more smartphones and more time on social media," according to San Diego State University professor and psychologist Jean Twenge. After seeing posts that trumpet their friends' successes, many teens are prone to thinking that these friends lead "cooler," or more fun, lives than they do. They may envy those successes and compare themselves unfavorably, thus leading to feelings of depression. "This is not about taking the phone away," Twenge cautions parents. "They are wonderful devices, but it's limited use. Make sure the phone doesn't become an **appendage**."

Social media also cuts down on human

Though meant to be methods for sustaining connections with one another, ever-present devices may sometimes have isolating effects.

interactions. "Face-to-face conversation is the most human—and humanizing—thing we do," notes clinical psychologist Sherry Turkle. "But these days we find ways around conversation. We hide from each other even as we're constantly connected to each other."

Xfinity, an Internet provider, produced a TV commercial that exemplifies this falloff in conversation. It shows that families through the ages have always used dinnertime to discuss their lives. Then it cuts to a modern family. A man, boy, and girl are sitting at the dinner table, totally immersed in their own electronic devices. They

POINTING OUT

FAKE NEWS

In 2017, the official Collins Dictionary Word of the Year was "fake news." According to the fact-checking website PolitiFact, "Fake news is made-up stuff, masterfully manipulated to look like **credible** *journalistic reports that are easily spread online to large audiences willing to believe the fictions and spread the word." Many people believe that Facebook has played a key role in the spread of fake news. Users share stories, believing they are true. In turn, those stories rank higher in search engine results, further increasing their circulation. Both major political parties have claimed that the prevalence of fake news had a major effect on the 2016 U.S. presidential election.*

Social media can become a springboard for conversations when friends and families interact face-to-face as well as online.

Delete "Facebook"?

Deleting this app will also its data.

Cancel

Relieved of the pressure to check and post updates, a break from social media can help avid users refocus their attention on other aspects of their lives.

ignore the woman who begins to put food on the table. She uses a control that pauses the devices. They are momentarily startled at the interruption. The commercial ends when she sits down and asks, "How is everyone?" The message is clear: families need to devote time to interacting with one another without looking at their devices.

What is the solution? To some, it may involve abandoning social media. For most people, though, that is too radical. Some people have suggested government regulation of Facebook and other tech giants. But regulation can easily turn to censorship. "My hope is that we—meaning both the [social media] industry and all of us—will find a way to keep and improve on what we love precisely by being precise about what must be rejected," says virtual reality and social media expert Jaron Lanier. "The world is changing rapidly under our command, so doing nothing is not an option."

There can be no question that the rise of social media has been a turning point in history. Certainly it is has had far-ranging effects on our daily lives. We can hope that in the future, people will continue to find ways to enhance the benefits of social media while limiting its negative effects.

1840s	The telegraph begins widespread operations in the U.S. and establishes many of the conventions used in modern social media.
March 10, 1876	Alexander Graham Bell has the first telephone conversation on the device he invented.
1969	ARPANET is established and becomes the foundation of the Internet.
1980s	Personal computers become increasingly popular.
1990s	E-mail becomes widely used.
1993	The World Wide Web transforms the Internet.
1997	SixDegrees.com becomes the first popular social networking site.
2002	Friendster is launched and quickly attracts 3 million users.
2003	MySpace is founded and soon replaces Friendster as the most popular social media site.
February 2004	Harvard student Mark Zuckerberg establishes The Facebook.
February 14, 2005	YouTube is founded; Google purchases the video sharing website less than two years later.
2006	Twitter is founded; Zuckerberg opens what is now Facebook to anyone 13 and older with a valid e-mail address.
2008	Facebook overtakes MySpace as the most popular social networking site.
October 6, 2010	Instagram is founded; Facebook purchases it two years later.
May 18, 2012	Facebook becomes a publicly traded company.
2017	Twitter doubles its allowable number of characters, from 140 to 280.
2018	Facebook faces several congressional inquiries about user privacy and other concerns.

anti-Semitism—prejudice against Jews

appendage—something attached to a larger entity; in humans refers to arms, legs, or other body parts

caroms—strikes against and rebounds

credible—believable, convincing

debunked—proved to be false

dial-up—using phone lines to establish an Internet connection

dormitory—a building with bedrooms in a school or other institution

entrepreneurs—people who plan and organize a new business, usually with substantial financial risk

extremists–people who believe in using violence or other extreme measures to enforce uncompromising views

fledgling—something that is just starting out and is not yet fully developed

genre—a category of artistic composition

haberdashers—dealers in men's clothing and accessories

magistrate—a public official who administers the law, which includes the ability to perform marriages

maritime—relating to the seas

regimes—rules of specific governments or leaders, usually oppressive

Roman Forum—in ancient Rome, the central area serving as a public gathering place and containing government buildings and open-air markets

susceptible—likely to be influenced by a particular thing or idea

telegraph—an electrical system for transmitting messages from distance along wire

template—an overall pattern

transatlantic—crossing the Atlantic Ocean

Bernstein, William J. *Masters of the Word: How Media Shaped History from the Alphabet to the Internet.* New York: Grove Press, 2013.

Blossom, John. *Content Nation: Surviving and Thriving as Social Media Changes Our Work, Our Lives, and Our Future.* Indianapolis: Wiley, 2009.

Lanier, Jaron. *Ten Arguments for Deleting Your Social Media Accounts Right Now.* New York: Henry Holt, 2018.

Luttrell, Regina. *Social Media: How to Engage, Share, and Connect.* Lanham, Md.: Rowman & Littlefield, 2015.

O'Connor, Rory. *Friends, Followers, and the Future: How Social Media Are Changing Politics, Threatening Big Brands, and Killing Traditional Media.* San Francisco: City Lights Books, 2012.

Standage, Tom. *Writing on the Wall: Social Media—The First 2,000 Years.* New York: Bloomsbury, 2013.

Turkle, Sherry. *Reclaiming Conversation: The Power of Talk in a Digital Age.* New York: Penguin, 2015.

Waters, John K. *The Everything Guide to Social Media.* Avon, Mass.: Adams Media, 2010.

Internet Matters: Social Media Networks Made for Children
*https://www.internetmatters.org/hub/news-blogs/social-media-networks
-made-for-kids/*
Learn about social networks with demonstrated safety records.

Safe Search Kids: A Teen's Guide to Social Media Safety
*https://www.safesearchkids.com/a-teens-guide-to-social-media-safety
/#.XE9BFi2ZNjQ*
Read these tips for staying safe while using social media.

Note: Every effort has been made to ensure that the websites listed above are suitable for children, that they have educational value, and that they contain no inappropriate material. However, because of the nature of the Internet, it is impossible to guarantee that these sites will remain active indefinitely or that their contents will not be altered.

INDEX